D0343257

RUNNING FOR THE SOUL

STORIES OF TRIUMPH, LAUGHTER,
COURAGE, SIMPLE PLEASURES
AND DREAMS FULFILLED

EDITED BY CLAUDIA PIEPENBURG, **ROAD RUNNER SPORTS**®

RUNNING FOR THE SOUL

Acknowledgments

This book has truly been a labor of love that would not have been possible without the help of many dedicated people. Thanks to Don Purviance for his critical editorial assistance, and Claudia Cunningham and Joan Maloney for their superb design work. I'd also like to thank the employees at Road Runner Sports who've supported me throughout this project.

Most of all, I want to thank all the wonderful people I've come to know during the past several months. Their willingness to share their stories has made this book possible.

RUNNING FOR THE SOUL

I recently spent a pleasant hour or so with this manuscript. The mix of runners most of us know and little-known people we can identify with, and the blend of stories by the athletes and stories written about others, makes easy and inspiring reading.

Joe Henderson
longtime running
columnist, author of
several books, speaker.

My favorite story is the one about the runner whose dream was to live to enjoy spending time with his grandchild. I loved his phrase: "I learned that your vision calls you forward — discipline drives you."

Bill Rodgers
Four-time winner of the
Boston and New York City
Marathons; the most
widely recognized and
well-loved distance
runner in the world.

Motive,

Motivation,

to Motivate

We use these words often: "What's your motive for making that decision?" "Where do you get the motivation to do the things you do?" "What can I do to motivate myself?"

The dictionary defines "motive" 1. as noun. (from the Latin movere, to move) An inner drive, impulse, etc. that causes one to act; incentive 2. (MOTIF)-adjective meaning of or causing motion.

That's it, a combination of numbers one and two — the inner drive that causes motion! And that motion, that movement, is...simply, running.

"What's your motive for deciding to quit smoking and start running?" "Where do you get the motivation to get up at 5:30 six days a week and run four miles before work?" "What can I do to get myself motivated to start racing again?" Now you understand where we're headed.

In this book we'll define motivation in many ways. The motivation to run is as individual and unique as the runner. Everyone has a distinct story, a different reason, and a singular inner drive. Some of the stories will make you laugh. Some will make you cry. All will make you marvel at the tenacity, strength and infinite beauty of the human spirit. Interspersed among the stories you'll find small gems of wisdom. You'll find quotes, tips and suggestions from the famous and not so famous. You'll also find words to make you think about what motivates you, words to make you search even deeper within yourself to discover your own inner drive.

We hope we've motivated you to turn the pages and begin your journey of discovery. You'll want to make stops along the way. This isn't a pilgrimage you'll make hastily. Read a few stories and take time to relish what you've read. Mark the pages you'll want to return to again and again, and write down the quotes that have special meaning for you.

Every run, every journey, begins with the first step...

Claudia Piepenburg

CLAUDIA PIEPENBURG — EDITOR

RUNNING FOR THE SOUL

Father's Day Run

"C'mon, Daddy. We've got to run." The voice of Catherine, my five-year-old daughter echoed in my head as I ran. It was Father's Day morning. The day was gorgeous, magnificently sunny with a light northerly breeze that brought a slight chill to the early morning air. June in Alabama such days are rare. It was the kind of morning for a mind-expanding run. During the run my mind kept replaying some of the events of the last few weeks. Being Father's Day, my mind wandered to my children.

Four weeks earlier Catherine had begun to take a major interest in running. Until then, she had faithfully waited while I circled the loop of my training run. She had watched me run races. She had even tried running a few times herself. Then suddenly she began inviting me to run with her. Our running relationship had reached a new level. As I reflected, so had our familial relationship.

"C'mon, Daddy!" Her voice echoed again as I recalled her coaxing me off the couch that first Sunday afternoon. She was bringing my shoes to me. Hers were already on. She had mapped out our route, a circuitous squiggle drawn on a page torn out of her coloring book. She insisted I carry it so we wouldn't get lost. I consulted the map, then my daughter and I began our first training run together.

"C'mon Daddy. We've got to run."

I was surprised at how well she did. Her smiling determination never faltered as we covered almost one mile in about nine minutes. Her time would have been better if we hadn't stopped to look at the bunny rabbit that crossed the road in front of us. Catherine was actually very good for her age. My vision, clouded by paternal pride, began imagining her leading her class to the finish in her kindergarten running contests. The Alabama state record in the mile for five year olds was well within her reach. Of course a trophy case would be needed before the end of the year. I stroked my parental ego and without realizing it, tried to impart my desires for success on her when all she wanted was to spend time with her daddy. I had come very close to making a mistake.

Four weeks later, on that beautiful Father's Day morning run, I was smiling at all the fatherly thoughts I'd been having and was glad I'd come to my senses.

Just the day before we'd run in a local event, a 5K for adults and a kids' mile. The mile race offered age-group medals. I had briefly slipped into my fatherly frame of mind and daydreamed of Catherine outrunning every five and six year old in Birmingham. But my good sense prevailed, and my family and I had arrived at the race expecting nothing more than having a good time. Anything else would have ruined the fun for Catherine and me.

I ran the 5K and was soundly defeated by thirty other runners. Then we prepared for the feature race: the kid's one-mile. Catherine and I lined up to run together. I was nervous and my heart was pounding. She seemed more interested in the Birmingham Bull's mascot rollicking among the runners than the race. The gun sounded and thirty children ages thirteen and under took off on a surprisingly difficult, hilly course. Catherine showed her usually radiant resolve. I allowed her to set her own pace, but supplied ample encouragement. At the end, I sprinted ahead to photograph her finish. My hug circled her neck like a medal and our mutual smiles would have been ample reward for what we'd done.

But Catherine had won! Her 9:58 beat all the other five and six year olds. She accepted the gold medal, and teased her daddy because he didn't have one. Then we all went to the zoo and enjoyed the day. We had spent a wonderful weekend together and built a priceless memory.

As I recalled all that had happened on that day, in the midst of my run my smile broadened, my legs moved a little faster and my heart swelled as though I had reached the elusive "runner's high." Actually, I was high on something more substantial — my family.

Blane Schilling
Carrollton, AL

"The great thing in this world
is not so much where we are,
but in what direction we are moving."
OLIVER WENDALL HOLMES

Breakfast
is Good

For over twenty years, the women's division of our Hartford Track Club of Hartford, Connecticut, has held Saturday breakfast runs. We meet at someone's home at 7:00 a.m., run anywhere from three to six miles, and then enjoy coffee and breakfast. As many as thirty runners show up faithfully in rain, sleet, snow and heat. We are housewives, teachers, clergywomen, attorneys, physicians and businesswomen, and many of us are triathletes. We train for regional 5Ks, 10Ks, half-marathons and marathons. We're truly a celebration of fitness, running and life!

Caroline Lloyd
Hartford Track Club

*"I originated this group
and am very proud of it and them!"*

A Different Kind of Runner

Here are some of his numbers:

June, 1999 — Suzuki Rock 'n Roll Marathon,
          San Diego, CA–7:00
April, 2000 — Country Music Marathon,
          Nashville, TN–4:56
June, 2000 — Suzuki Rock 'n Roll Marathon-5:13

Now I'll tell you why I'm so impressed. His 1999 first-time-ever marathon in seven hours becomes even more special when you consider it came only eight weeks after his knee surgery and only five months after he began to train as a distance runner. In fact, his 2000 Rock 'n Roll finish would have been faster if he hadn't gone back to help his mother finish. (She was running in the 65–69 age division.) Then there were his two half-marathon finishes, one the Santa Barbara Pier to Peak, which rises nearly 4,000 feet in elevation.

To put all this in further perspective, you need to know more about Joseph Cochran. Joe smokes, although he knows he could run faster if he'd only quit. He also drinks lots of beer and never trains between races. Joe's style is to run as hard as he can for as long as possible, walk to recover, then run hard again and so on throughout the entire race. He ran his first short race in jeans and boots, and his racing trademark is a broad-brimmed, dark-brown, felt cowboy hat. Why the cowboy hat? Joe says it's in celebration of his high school days as a bull rider in county rodeos.

I got to talking with Joe when he began to key off me during races. He would walk until I caught up with him, then surge ahead until he became winded, at which point he'd resume walking until I came up alongside of him. Once I pulled up next to him, he would spurt off quickly again.

"Joe's style is to run as hard as he can for as long as possible, walk to recover, then run hard again and so on throughout the entire race."

Joe now works as a deckhand on a sea urchin boat. All of his on-land transportation is by bicycle or on foot, and his distance running gives him the opportunity to be with his mom. What's next for the mother-son duo? The St. George and Berlin Marathons.

Told by Ralph Philbrick
Santa Barbara, California

Birthday Mile:

April 24, 1985

It's four days short of four months since the accident. I've spent two months in traction and six weeks in a body cast. I'm currently sporting a brace made of metal and leather. It's a definite improvement over the mummy look of my days in the cast and considerably more comfortable. I'm even allowed to remove the brace for twenty-minute intervals a few times a day so I can begin strengthening the muscles holding up my head. I still need to wear a soft collar when I'm not wearing the brace, although I can manage the totally naked neck long enough to get in a quick shower.

I'm thirty years old today and I know exactly what present I want to give myself. I call my sister Linda and ask her to take me to the track. I want her to pace me through a mile in 7:30. She agrees without hesitation and without questioning my sanity, which I deeply appreciate.

For the first time in months I open my running closet, and the memories and emotions stirred by the assortment of T-shirts and shorts is over-whelming. If you've ever abruptly realized that you're repeating a routine that's become second nature, you'll understand how I'm feeling as it occurs to me that I'm dressing again in time-hon-ored sequence. As I lace up my shoes and strap on my watch, I can feel myself transforming from a broken-neck person into a runner.

"I'm thirty years old today
and I know exactly what present
I want to give myself."

Linda arrives, and we drive to the university and park behind the field house. Strolling over to the track, as we have so many times before, we're filled with the nervous excitement that precedes a track workout. As we go through the pre-workout stretching routine, we discuss the best strategy to accomplish our goal of running a 7:30 mile. We decide that maintaining an even pace is the best strategy, and I tell Linda that, if I'm feeling good with a lap to go, I'll signal her to drop the pace and see if we can slip under 7:30.

We clear our watches and toe the start line. Linda gets us to the quarter right on pace. I feel a little awkward because my upper body moves like it's still in a cast. But my legs feel strong and fluid. We hit the half in 3:45; Linda always was good at pacing. I know my form must look pathetic, but in my mind's eye I'm running smooth and strong. As we come around for the third lap I give Linda the go ahead to drop the pace. We kick in the final quarter and finish in a time of 7:27.

"Well, that's a start. One mile in 7:27. I've got three years until the Olympic Trials; I'll need to run twenty-six of those back to back about ninety seconds per mile faster," I say between gasps. This seems to be a realistic possibility. I look up at Linda and she's nodding her head. "Yeah, Jane, you can do that." We slowly turn away from the track and walk back past the field house to the parking lot, veterans of another track session, dreaming of races to come.

Jane Welzel
Ft. Collins, CO

Postscript: In the 1988 Olympic Marathon Trials I finished 13th overall in a time of 2:36:08 (5:57 per mile).

Editors Note: In December 1984 Jane Welzel was involved in a serious automobile accident. Prior to the accident she had been one of the most successful women runners in the country. The accident, which nearly ended her life, broke her neck in nine places. Doctors told her she might never walk again, let alone run. Determined to prove them wrong, she fought against the odds and emerged as a top-ranked open runner through the late 1980s and well into the 1990s. She won the USA National Marathon Championships in 1990, was ninth at the 1992 Olympic Trials Marathon, and competed at the World Championships Marathon in 1993. In 1995 she turned forty. For the past five years she has been ranked as one of the top five masters women athletes in the United States. In 2000, at the age of forty-four, she competed in her fifth Olympic Trials Marathon.

July 4, 1998, 7:18 p.m.
Frederick, Maryland

What was my motivation to start training and racing again as a masters runner? I remember it well. The occasion was in 1998, a Fourth of July race in Frederick, Maryland. An eleven-year-old kid passed me at the one-mile mark in a 5K and beat me. He ran 17:45. I ran 18:20. I realized then that I should quit playing hockey and seriously train — or quit racing forever. I realized that kids, little kids, and even most big kids, shouldn't be beating me!

Steve Nearman
Alexandria, VA

"Winning isn't everything.
Wanting to win is."
CATFISH HUNTER

Paul Greer's Running Tips

How do I keep my athletes motivated? Here are a few of the "pep talks" I've given to runners over the years.

- Keep in mind that everyone improves at a different rate. Some people can jog for an hour after four weeks of training, while others may take four months or even a year to reach that point. Don't get discouraged. Continue to listen to your own body. Eventually you'll get there.

- Your reward for running done gradually, comfortably, and pleasantly will be a new life. You'll feel better mentally, and you'll both look and feel better physically.

- Think of training and exercise in terms of frequency rather than intensity — and in terms of pleasure rather than pain. Use exercise as a reward.

- Run against the wind on the way out and with the wind on the way back.

- Muscles weigh more than fat. While you may not lose pounds, you'll lose inches.

- At fifty beats per minute, an athlete's heart beats thirteen million fewer times per year than if it were pumping at a normal seventy-five beats per minute.

- Always remember that exercise is cumulative, so look for the long-term effects.

- Finally, think positive thoughts, and you'll improve.

"You cannot make someone exercise;
however,
if you paint a pretty enough picture,
and the athlete buys into that picture,
that is motivation."

PAUL GREER

Paul Greer is the coach of the San Diego Track Club and the cross-country coach at San Diego City College. He ran a 3:39 1,500 at the 1992 Olympic Trials.

When the Word "Hero" isn't Enough

Heroes are hard to come by these days. In these times of victimization, rampant lawsuits, co-dependency and passing the buck, most people are hard-pressed to name their heroes. Few folks can think of anyone; at least, no one they've heard or read about who seems to measure up. Occasionally, someone will mention a former teacher or perhaps even a military figure; after all, the dictionary definition suggests that a hero is any person, especially a man, admired for courage, nobility, etc. But is it the definition that's lacking, or is it the lack of people who fit the description? After meeting Marla Runyan, I've come to the conclusion that the answer is a little bit of both.

The first time I saw Marla, she was running in a race, the Carlsbad 5000, her first competition on the road. I'd seen photos of her, so I knew I'd be able to spot her when she ran by. No more than fifteen women participate in this elite race, but even in a larger field I could have immediately picked her out. Marla is tall, her legs are long and incredibly well-muscled and she runs straight-backed, with her head held high and her stride extended. She's a powerful runner, powerful yet not intimidating, exhibiting as much grace as power. Watching her run, I was struck by how calm she looked, how very calm and peaceful. Marla's face belied her five-minute-per-mile pace; she might have been quietly meditating.

The second time I saw Marla was after the race, when she was sitting in the lobby of her hotel. She was comfortably curled into a Queen Anne chair, and, with what appeared to be a microscopic lens, was closely studying a menu. For a few brief seconds I was struck by the dichotomy, the stark contrast between the Marla I'd seen running just a few hours before and this woman who was openly trying to decipher a menu. Within the blink of an eye, my initial reaction was forgotten. What the eyes see is often not the whole picture.

"...the dictionary definition suggests that a hero is any person, especially a man, admired for courage, nobility, etc. But is it the definition that's lacking..."

Marla and I spent the next hour together, sitting side by side on a sofa in the lobby where she told me her story. Up close her face seemed more chiseled and angular, the skin stretched tightly across high cheekbones. Even in repose, she reminded me of a cheetah, strong, powerful and able to instantly spring into action. I sensed that, at any moment, she might uncoil her legs, stretch out her torso, and take off on a run. She had a strong voice, strong and confident; she didn't flinch at any questions, but answered without hesitation. During our conversation, her hazel eyes seldom moved and focused on a point slightly to the left of my left eyebrow. I returned her gaze, looking into her eyes throughout the hour, making contact even though I knew she couldn't see where I was looking. Our two sets of eyes were both registering limited perceptions, were both missing the whole picture. Over the course of our visit, however, my eyes came to truly see. I came to know who Marla Runyan really is, I discovered a new meaning of the word "hero," and the picture became whole.

"Marla the athlete has always taken precedence over Marla the blind runner."

Much has been written about Marla since she qualified for the 2000 Summer Olympics. Writers and reporters focus, rightly so, on the fact that she's legally blind and that, before making the Olympic team in the 1,500-meter run, she competed in the Paralympics. People read or hear her story, and, again, rightly so, they're moved by the fact that a woman who can see only shapes and colors, who can't see to drive, who can't read without a special magnifying lens, and who can't see to the end of the straightaway on the track, somehow managed to race against the best women runners in the country and qualify for the Olympics. Marla's story is indeed inspirational, not so much because she's triumphed over what appears to be adversity, but because of the way she sees herself and the way she wants others to see her.

We didn't talk long about her eyesight; Marla wanted to get on with telling me about the love she has for her sport and the goals she's set for herself. The longer we spoke, the more I began to understand what a very small part her limited sight plays in her life. Marla the athlete has always taken precedence over Marla the blind runner. She began our interview by telling me that she'd been an athlete since childhood, beginning with soccer when she was only six. Her schedule soon expanded to include gymnastics and swimming, so that her childhood revolved around the playing fields, the field house or the pool. Marla's gradual loss of vision didn't stop her from doing any of the things she loved. It was her parents who suffered, whose lives were in a constant state of upheaval. One doctor told them that Marla would grow out of it, that she was suffering from a psychosomatic disorder brought on by watching the television character Mary going blind on the show, "The Little House on the Prairie." Another doctor told them Marla would be totally blind before she reached her teens.

Marla didn't grow out of the condition, nor did she go totally blind. Staargard's disease, a form of macular degeneration, left her with uncorrectable 20/400 vision. She's limited to peripheral vision, so that the central portion of her view of the world is forever clouded. When she looks at you, she can't see your face, and when she runs, she can make out only shapes of the runners around her; she can tell what colors they're wearing, but can't read their bib numbers. She knows her opponents by the sound of their breathing, she knows what color hair they have, and she knows how their voices sound. When she races on the track, she's more comfortable being among the pack, and when she gets out in front, there's nothing but the seemingly endless red blur of track, striped with white lanes, resembling some sort of wild, impressionistic painting of indistinct colors. Those are the times she comes face to face with her limitations, the times she realizes her opponents are seeing so much more; it's then that Marla reminds herself, "I belong here."

Marla does belong, and, to be where she is today, she has worked long and hard at the sport she loves. In high school she competed in the high jump and 100 meters, and still holds her school's record in the high jump. San Diego State

University recruited Marla as a high jumper, and she later went on to represent that school by competing in the mile relay. As a college junior, she decided to try the heptathalon, figuring she'd be good at it. She was so good that she finished tenth at the 1996 Olympic Track and Field Trials. In preparation for the trials, Marla fashioned herself into an incredibly muscular and strong athlete through a grueling regimen of training, including hours of jumping, throwing and sprinting, day after day. When she set an American heptathlon record in the 800 meters at the trials, Marla knew she was on the verge of a breakthrough. She decided that it was time to move on to new challenges, that she would become a middle distance runner.

"I belong here."

It's rare for an athlete to switch from the heptathlon to distance running. The heptathlon requires sheer strength and power, while distance running demands primarily speed. For Marla the transition wasn't easy. In 1996, she relocated to Eugene, Oregon, to be near her coach and have the opportunity to train with other middle distance runners. A month after arriving she had knee surgery, and, during the next two years she suffered a succession of one injury after another. Anyone else might have given up, moved back home and let go of her dream, but not Marla.

"...*why worry about something I can't control?*"

Marla doesn't ever make excuses, and she doesn't ever ask for pity. Not once while she told me her amazing story did she ever utter the words, "why me?" Such phrases simply aren't in her vocabulary. She wants no one to feel sorry for her, because she has never once in her life felt sorry for herself. She's never felt sorry for herself for not being able to see what others see, never felt sorry for herself for her proclivity to sustain injuries. She knew that, if she left Eugene, she'd be giving up, giving up her dream of racing on the track, even giving up running, the one thing she wanted to do more than anything else in her life. So, rather than giving up, she briefly "let go" of her dream and ran for the reasons she'd always run, because she loved it. She had to start training all over again; she'd missed two years and was no farther along than she'd been when she first moved to Oregon. But it was all right... because she could run again.

Run she did. In 1999, she set the second fastest American 1,500 meters time for women. Early in 2000, she won the 3,000 meters at the U.S. Indoor Track and Field Championships. And on that cool afternoon when she ran the Carlsbad 5000, she finished fifth overall, fifth in a field that included former Olympians and world- and national-class athletes.

As excited as Marla was about her finish in the race earlier that day, she made it clear that she had much bigger goals. She had qualified for the Olympic Trials 1,500 meters. The next four months would mean harder training, long runs on trails with marathoners and 10K runners, time trials on the road, and weight work. I asked her if it wasn't difficult to do hard runs on trails; didn't she worry about tripping or about bumping into another runner? She said, "No. Why worry about something I can't control? My vision is the way things are. I accept it. People often ask me how I manage to do what I do. They're guessing at what it must be like for me. They're overestimating or underestimating what I can or can't see. They'll never know, and it doesn't matter. What matters is that I accept it. It's the way it is." We stood, our conversation was over, and I instinctively held out my hand. For a brief instant Marla didn't move. Then her right arm shot out, and she firmly gripped my hand. She smiled. I smiled back and I said, "I'll be watching you in the Olympics."

Of course, Marla did make it to the Olympics, but it wasn't easy. She barely made qualifying at the trials. While on a training run just a few days before the meet, she pulled a muscle when she jumped out of the way of a child riding a bike on the trail. She was already suffering from an injury she'd sustained a few weeks earlier when she stepped off a curb. Despite the fact that she couldn't even do a warm-up prior to her race, she qualified for the Olympic 1,500-meter team and was on her way to Sydney. It was there that Marla demonstrated so clearly what a true champion she is and why she's a hero. During an interview shortly before the final, Marla said that she'd do anything she could to help her teammate, Suzy Favor-Hamilton, win a medal. While other athletes were bragging to the press about how great they were and about how many medals they'd won or were going to win, Marla was indicating her willingness to help someone else win a medal. Realistically, she knew that she wasn't as fast as many of the other women in the field, and that gold, silver or bronze medals weren't in her future, but she would selflessly do what she could so another runner could achieve her dream. She got her chance. The first lap of the 1,500 meters was surprisingly slow, too slow in fact for an Olympic final. Sensing that the pace needed picking up, Marla moved to the front of the pack shortly after the first lap, knowing that Favor-Hamilton would follow her and move into medal position.

Watching Marla as she doggedly moved to the front, I tried to imagine what was going through her mind at that moment. I couldn't imagine what it looked like for her, that long expanse of red, striated with white, surrounded by an audience of multi-colored blobs. I tried to imagine what the sound must have been like, but it was impossible. Watching Marla race again, I knew that, although I could never feel what she feels, see how she sees, or hear what she hears, it didn't matter because I was seeing her for who and what she is — a hero. Without question, Marla is courageous and noble, but she's even more than that. She's also totally selfless and has never offered an excuse; for Marla, there simply are no excuses. Watching her that night, I imagined that she was thinking, "I belong here."

"What our eyes see is often not the whole picture."

The day of our interview, Marla had asked me where she and her boyfriend should go for dinner. That's why she'd been reading the hotel restaurant menu when I arrived. She told me they preferred someplace with "really good seafood" and added that she wanted a restaurant that "overlooked the ocean." I recommended a popular spot just down the coast, a restaurant that featured windows along one side and facing out to sea. It wasn't until several months later that it suddenly occurred to me that Marla couldn't have seen the ocean. And I realized that it didn't matter. What our eyes see is often not the whole picture.

Always Look Forward to Tomorrow!

Running is a way of life for me. In the mid-seventies, I started running marathons and eventually completed thirty-five of them. Besides marathons, I ran many shorter distance races in more than a dozen states around the country, from Boston to Atlanta and as far west as Pike's Peak in Colorado Springs. Training for all these races was exhilarating. Often alone, I allowed my thoughts to flow free while I reveled in the pleasures that come with physical activity. My motivation to run came from deep within.

About ten years ago, I became intrigued with ultra-running. Running on trails through often-desolate areas has provided me with a whole new set of physical challenges, as well as with different mental and emotional challenges from those I'd faced before. I usually do ultra-runs of 50K (thirty-one miles) or more. The courses are generally over rough terrain and in the woods with the associated eerie sounds. Since I'm slow, I'm usually running in virtual isolation with no other runners in sight. All I have to occupy my mind are the animal sounds to hear and respond to and my own thoughts. Besides being slow, I have a propensity for getting lost. A $2 investment in a compass helped instill some confidence! Still, I've had some horrific experiences, like vomiting from ingesting sickening fluid replacement drinks and then suffering terrible weakness when I was still miles from civilization.

Unlike shorter distance races, I seldom complete these ultra-runs. Usually I retire at a checkpoint some fifteen to twenty miles into the event, but that's okay with me. I always say to myself, "There's a next time."

I learn from each event and vow to do things differently during the next ultra-run. The severe blisters, knee pain, stomach problems and bad shoes have all combined to make ultras a new and supreme challenge that I will not retreat from until the day I die. I don't care what might come next, what potential roadblocks might be out there and standing in my way of completing the distance. I intend to continue to compete within myself as long as I'm alive. I'm fifty-four now, and I'm confident that my future holds many more runs!

I hope others will maintain the same faith in themselves as I have in myself. I hope people will continue to set individual goals and strive to achieve them. I tell people not to ever look back. One or two steps backward is only temporary, so always look forward. I believe that, as a runner, being a self-motivator and self-achiever spills over into every facet of life. Live my motto: LOOK FORWARD TO TOMORROW!

Gary Glaser
Lexington Park, MD

Train Right, and Trust in God

In April 1999, Catherine Ndereba ran her first marathon, the Boston Marathon, and was the sixth woman to cross the finish line. The very next year her first-place finish stunned her competition and the world. Although she won nearly every race she ran during the second half of 1999, her victory in Boston was a surprise to everyone, except, perhaps, to Catherine herself.

Even though she'd run as a young schoolgirl in her native Kenya, Catherine never realized until later in her life that she had exceptional talent for running. In those days Catherine's father, also a runner, had encouraged her to compete, and her personal objective had simply been to run hard enough "to beat the boys." She accomplished that objective by often beating the boys, but her times weren't particularly fast. Fast or not, she loved to run, and, in 1994, she ran in the World Junior Cross-country Championships and finished twentieth.

While she was in college, Catherine continued competing and won many major road races in the U.S., but wasn't named to the 1999 World Cross-country Championships Kenyan team. Disappointed, yet eager to prove herself, she convinced her agent to get her an entry into the Boston Marathon. Since her training hadn't been geared to the marathon distance, her coach was surprised to learn Catherine planned to enter the Boston event.

The Boston course, however, afforded no surprises for Catherine because she'd already heard it was a challenge. Her goal, like that of so many other runners, was merely to finish, particularly since she'd only decided to run at the last minute. Through the first seventeen miles she felt great, but began to falter on the infamous "Heartbreak Hill" portion of the course. From mile nineteen through the finish, Catherine grimly persisted and did her best, because she had, after all, vowed to finish no matter what!

Catherine couldn't sleep at all the night after the race. She kept replaying it again and again in her mind, thinking about how much better she would have run if only she'd properly trained.

When the day dawned for the 2000 Boston Marathon, Catherine was ready. Her experience the previous year had taught her how to train specifically to race the Boston course. Catherine's game plan was to run according to how her body would feel on race day. She started the race with confidence based on her 1999 experience and with the determination to do her very best. She simply put her faith in God and trusted that she would "pay the price," one way or another. The pay off was a win in the most famous marathon in the world.

Catherine's story provides a good example for every runner. Even the best runners in the world face the same challenges as do the middle- and back-of-the-pack athletes.

Catherine's suggestions for distance runners:

- Sometimes you'll face setbacks. Don't let them get you down. Find a way around them.

- "Just finishing" is a worthy goal.

- You run your first marathon. You race your second.

- Train for the course. Train hard. Train smart.

- Your body will let you know how to run.

- Trust in yourself, and have faith.

Catherine Ndereba was the number one ranked female distance runner in the world in 1996, 1998, and 1999. (She was on maternity leave in 1997). Besides the Boston Marathon, her first-place finishes include the Utica Boilermaker 15K, Examiner Bay to Breakers 12K, Quad-City Times X-Bix 7 Mile, Falmouth Road Race 7.1 Mile, and the Crim Festival of Races 10 Mile. She was second in the 1999 New York City Marathon.

Envisioning a New Person
by Envisioning the Finish Line

JEFFREY WANCHENA'S STORY

He still hears the taunts and the laughter. When Jeffrey Wanchena was a 300-pound high school student, he had to run a lap around the track in his physical education class. He remembers the other students laughing at the huge, lumbering young man as he tried to finish. He remembers the physical and psychological pain. In fact, much of what Jeffrey remembers about the first three-quarters of his life is constant shame, guilt and humiliation.

The facts of Jeffrey's life read like something out of a Charles Dickens novel. He suffered physical abuse from a close family member when he was only a youngster. Retreating into his own world to escape the hurt, he became a compulsive overeater. In the first grade he already weighed over 100 pounds. Three times before the age of eighteen he tried grueling water fasts to take off the weight and once lost 120 pounds. Sadly, he gained it back within a few months. He drank and smoked throughout his adolescence and says now that "were it not for God's grace I would have been dead or in jail." He continued to abuse his body into adulthood. By the time he was forty-five, Jeffrey weighed 420 pounds.

"To commit, we all need to have a vision of our real selves."

It was the impending birth of his first grandchild that made him reflect on his condition, and eventually turn his life around. "I knew if I was going to see my grandchild grow up, I had to deal with the issues that had confronted me all my life. I came to the realization that I didn't have to accept that my past history defined me. Instead I decided it obscured the real me."

The real Jeffrey wasn't an obese, compulsive over-eater, unable to control his appetites. The real Jeffrey was a strong, healthy man crossing a finish line, feeling like "the king of the world." In late 1994, Jeffrey began to walk. "I couldn't afford a health club, but I could afford shoes and a rain suit." He walked twice a day for over a year. Then he began to jog. He found support in his family "for the things I was going to do with my life." He bought running books and subscribed to running magazines. He found a coach, learned how to stretch correctly and began to use a heart-rate monitor. He changed his eating habits. By the time his grandchild was born, he had lost his first 100 pounds. Months passed, the pounds disappeared, and the finish line was in sight.

"I learned that your vision calls you forward — discipline drives you. I believe there are no excuses. Day after day, no matter the weather I'm out there. When I was young I was always looking for short cuts, the easy way out. But there's no easy way. To commit, we all need to have a vision of our real selves. Over time, that vision can become reality."

Jeffrey's journey to his finish line took more than two years; in fact it took precisely five hours and forty-one minutes more than two years. In October 1997, he ran the Twin Cities Marathon in 5:41. He weighed 250 pounds at the time. He ran two marathons in 1998 and two more in 1999. Grandma's Marathon in 1999 was special. His twenty-four-year-old daughter ran with him. Although she finished in front of her dad, when she saw him coming toward the finish line, she jumped several barriers to join him. They crossed the line together, hands joined and arms raised in the triumph of the moment. The taunting of the overweight high school boy was, in that moment, muffled by the cheers of the spectators.

"When people hear my story, they think I'm some sort of extraordinary person who's accomplished things they could never do. That misses the mark.

I'm simply a human being who has used ordinary means to realize extraordinary healing. Those means are available to everyone, not just me. I had a vision of myself, of the person I knew I really was and could be. So, when I meet people who think that I'm somehow exceptional, I ask them, where do you want to be? Who do you envision yourself to be? The journey is central to the destination. See yourself as you want to be, then you'll know how to get there, to your own personal finish line."

"I learned that your vision calls you forward — discipline drives you."

Motivated for 25 Years!

I've been running for over twenty-five years. I first started shortly after college. The main reason I did it was to "get out and get physical." It made me feel good when I improved. Initially improvement was my motivation: running two miles, then three, five, seven and even up to ten.

After twenty-five years I've learned that your motivations to run can, and do, change. Here are the things that have kept me going all these years.

- Getting in shape for a particular race (in my case it was always Al's Run in Milwaukee, WI)

- Training to run a marathon

- Escape from the devastation of a divorce

- Running with people who saw me as a runner, as their equal, someone with the same physical goal

I guess you could say I'm addicted to running and that's okay. I've met so many people over the years who have the same wonderful "addiction" as I do. I've made many friends in my running years. It's fun to talk about what race we're training for and then root each other on. It's fun to talk about our past experiences. I get motivated just meeting my running buddies at a designated location, at a designated time, to run a designated distance!

I've always liked this phrase: SMILE at your neighbor and your neighbor will SMILE back. How about this for a paraphrase? SMILE at a runner,and a runner will ALWAYS SMILE BACK!

Tom Baas,
Member Badgerland
Striders,
Port Washington, WI

"Do what you can,
with what you have,
where you are."
THEODORE ROOSEVELT

Never Stop Dreaming

EMILY MARKERT'S STORY

While Emily Markert was in the hospital, dreaming of the day she'd be healthy again, she started walking back and forth, back and forth in her room, counting the steps. Her exercise range was circumscribed by linkage to the chest tubes that kept her lungs from collapsing. So she walked, baby steps back and forth, back and forth across the tiny room, her home for five months.

"I liked the way running made me feel."

Emily never expected to be in the hospital. Until June 1999, she was a healthy high school student who ran both track and cross-country. Since early childhood, running had been an important part of her life. In her soft, nearly tremulous voice she often describes her recollection of running in elementary school, "It was fun. You know how they had you try to run a mile? Some of the other kids didn't want to do it, but it felt good to me. I liked the way running made me feel."

She ran at every opportunity in elementary school and into middle school. When she was a freshman and sophomore in high school, she ran the mile, 800 meters, and cross-country, but started having trouble in her junior year. First it was anemia. "I was so tired all the time, and I wasn't running well. After the cross-country season, I found out I was anemic. I kept getting sick. Finally I had to have a transfusion." With the track season lost, Emily focused on getting ready for cross-country in the fall of her senior year. In June, she resumed training, but it wasn't long before she knew something was very, very wrong.

"I dreamt about being able to run again…"

Emily haltingly describes what she felt. "When I yawned, I got sharp pains. They were in my chest and back. I hurt, I knew something was really wrong, and I could feel — I could feel my heart beating fast. I remember the day I told my mom something wasn't right. She made an appointment for me to see the doctor on Monday. I didn't make it that long; we went to the emergency room right away."

On Monday, June 28, Emily was admitted to the hospital. On November 4, she finally left the hospital. She spent those five long months in four different facilities — two local hospitals, the Mayo Clinic, and the University of Southern California Medical Center. During the first few months, she passed the time by walking in her room to keep in shape while the doctors tried to determine exactly what was wrong. Emily figured she was eventually going to get better, so she worked hard at maintaining her fitness. "I kept thinking I was going to get better at any time, and I wanted to be ready." Little did she realize that, in order to get better, she was going to be faced with a physical and emotional challenge that few adults, let alone a seventeen-year-old high school student, could handle well.

In September, Emily's doctors told her and her family that she was going to need a lung transplant, a rarely performed surgery. Emily's illness, a highly uncommon form of pneumonia, had destroyed her lungs. Without the transplant, she would die. When she speaks of how she felt about the surgery, her voice rises with emotion. "I was really upset, you know? The whole idea of it upset me because I wanted to keep believing I'd get better without it, that the doctors could give me some kind of medicine to make me better. I knew the transplant meant that someone else was going to have to go through pain and lose part of themselves, and that bothered me."

Emily's mother, father, aunt and two uncles were considered as organ donors. The two uncles, Don and Larry Fitzgerald, were eventually chosen. During the six hours of surgery, a lobe was removed from the lung of each donor uncle and transplanted into Emily's chest. She matter-of-factly describes the procedure: "A normal lung has two lobes on the left and three on the right. Mine didn't work at all any more. So they took a lobe from Uncle Don and a lobe from Uncle Larry. My mom or dad would have been a good match, but their lungs weren't big enough."

The surgery was performed in California on October 15, and on December 2, Emily went home to Iowa. Determined to get back to running, she started jogging three months after returning home. It was a laborious process. "My muscles were so weak from all the medication I was taking. I had to start out by walking. Then I tried jogging, but I could only jog ten steps at a time. I dreamt about being able to run again, and when track started in the spring, I could finally jog a 200."

Although Emily wanted to train and compete with the team, the medications had taken a toll on her body. She developed stress fractures in both hips from steroids. When her doctor told her she couldn't run, determined to do anything she could to help the team, she volunteered to assist with timing. By the time the end of the season rolled around, she was able to start running again. "I ran the 200 in the last four meets of the season. I ran thirty-two seconds every time, but the last meet I ran my fastest split. It felt so good to be running again." Each time she raced, one of her uncles was there to watch her.

"I believe that what you put into something is what you get out of it."

On Saturday, August 5, ten months after the surgery, Emily competed in a local 5K. "I wanted to do it because I had run in the race before. While I was in the hospital, I'd thought about the race a lot. It meant so much to me to finish it. I'm still not strong, but my strength will come back. I know it will. I believe that what you put into something is what you get out of it." Emily has plans for a lot more running in her future. "I'm going to run the 5K again and compare my time to what I ran this year. I want to run longer distances so I can run with my sister. I'm never going to stop running." When asked what she enjoys about the sport, Emily quickly ticks off her answers. "The feeling of accomplishment I get when I've finished a run. You know — that good feeling; like wow, I just ran a mile! And running is good for my body. And it's relaxing. Well…it isn't always relaxing! But a lot of the time it is."

Emily started college in the fall of 2000; she's attending the local community college, but eventually she'll transfer to Iowa State. She's come a long, long way from that day when she first realized she was sick. The fact that she's alive is primarily due to the loving, totally selfless gift she received from her uncles. She acknowledges how truly lucky she is. "I'm so fortunate and so thankful for what my uncles did for me, but I feel sad for other people who are waiting for transplants. There are so many people who need them. Please, please let people know that being an organ donor is so important. Without an organ donation, I wouldn't be here today." With that thankful sentiment in mind, Emily Markert, daughter, granddaughter, sister, niece, college student, dreamer, and, oh, yes — runner — enters a new phase of her young and truly blessed life.

My Salvation

On November 4, 1980, I quit smoking and started jogging. I wasn't a heavy smoker, but I smoked enough that it was a monkey on my back. Without the harassment and encouragement of my former husband, Michael, I might still be a smoker. At the time Michael was a marathoner, Boston caliber. Needless to say, he was opposed to my smoking. He tried every way he could to convince me to stop smoking. Truthfully, I was tired of smoking my cigarettes secretly in the basement by the washer and dryer, but for fear I'd gain weight, I was afraid to quit.

Michael suggested I give up smoking by substituting it with a positive habit — jogging. He said all I needed was a good pair of running shoes, and I could run anytime, anywhere, either alone or with others. On November 2, I smoked only three cigarettes all day. On November 3, I smoked a morning and noon cigarette, then went out for my first jog that evening. I couldn't go far because

I had trouble breathing. On November 4, I didn't smoke all day. That night I jogged a block further than I had the evening before. Since that day twenty years ago, I've been a runner, not a smoker.

Running has rewarded me in many ways. I've become more conscious of my eating habits. I've run in many races over the years where I've met wonderful runners and made lifelong friends, I'm in excellent health, and I'm happy when I look in my closet and see all the shoes, running attire and race shirts.

Running has been my salvation.

Judy Harris
Washington, D.C.

"If we really want to live,
we'd better start at once to try."
W.H. AUDEN

Defying Death

RICHARD LEM'S STORY

The morning of the 2000 Los Angeles Marathon dawned cold, wet and windy. With temperatures in the high forties, winds gusting up to twenty-five miles an hour, and rain coming down sideways, the weather conditions could hardly have been described as "ideal" for a marathon. For the 366 runners who'd run in fourteen previous L.A. Marathons, the weather couldn't have been worse. To honor them, the race committee had invited these race veterans to line up behind the elite athletes at the front. Unfortunately, this meant being lined up and ready to run one full hour before the start time.

"It was pretty cold and wet, but I was just so happy to be there," Richard Lem admits. He was happy to be there because it meant another marathon, another day to do something for himself, something more spiritual than physical.

Richard has terminal cancer. Instead of focusing on his diseased body, he focuses on his spiritual side. He recognizes few people have a similar focus. "'Stop identifying with your body,' I tell people I meet. 'You're so much more than your body.'"

"...another marathon,

another day to do something for himself,

something more spiritual than physical."

Richard often talks with people suffering from cancer. "They're usually so depressed. So down, and they don't want to talk about it. I say, 'You have to talk about it! Talking is a catharsis.' I tell them to focus on something, anything to give them something to think about other than dying. You see, we're all dying. Some of us just take a different path to get there."

In high school and at Los Angeles City College, Richard ran hurdles, but couldn't make the team when he went on to UCLA. He'd started smoking while in the Army, and, by the time of his discharge, he'd stopped running altogether. Encouraged by a former Army buddy and Kenneth Cooper's aerobics book, he took up the sport again in 1965. "I ran with a vengeance, sometimes fifteen races a year." He was in his early thirties then, and, over the next decade, he became even more competitive. Running had become a way of life.

Richard was diagnosed with cancer of the prostate when he was sixty-four. The cancer spread rapidly to his ribs, shoulder blades and spine. Doctors also found a malignant tumor in his pancreas. They gave him a choice of treatments, standard chemotherapy or radical surgery. He opted for the chemotherapy. "I knew people had died during the surgery. I didn't want to miss running the L.A. Marathon. I figured that if I was going to die, I would rather die running on the streets of L.A. than in a hospital bed." The treatments made him weak, so he stopped them three months before the race. He finished the 1999 marathon three hours slower than his first one thirteen years earlier.

Richard attacks his disease on many levels. "I practice Xiang Gong (Chinese exercises to increase energy), get acupuncture treatments, take herbs, meditate twice a day and receive conventional cancer medications. I've learned through my illness that what's most important is developing a spiritual nature. We're all made up of many components: physical, mental, astral and spiritual. Running a marathon is all of those things."

He didn't dwell on the cancer before the 2000 race. "I didn't wonder if it might be my last. In fact, when I finished, my first thought was, 'Can I do better next time?' Because you never really know, do you? You don't know where the finish line is in life. Don't let dying dominate your life. Tomorrow might be the best day you'll ever experience."

Note: Richard has written a book titled "I'm Dying. But I'm Not Sick: The Final Journey". He finished the 2000 Los Angeles Marathon in 8:14:07.

"It's the steady,

constant driving to the goal

for which you're striving,

not the speed with which you travel,

that will make your victory sure."

ANONYMOUS

Steve Scott's Tips
for Staying Motivated

1. Always have a goal. It might be to beat your best previous time, or to race a different distance than you ever have before, or to lose ten pounds for a wedding (yours or someone else's). Or maybe your goal will be to run three miles instead of two, or even to run your first race or lower your blood pressure. No matter what your goal is — you need one. Without a goal, you won't train.

2. Reward yourself when you reach your goal. Set aside $1 each time you run. If you've achieved your goal at the end of a year (losing twenty pounds, for instance), buy yourself some new clothes or take a short trip with the money you've saved.

3. Find someone to run with. A running buddy holds you accountable. If you know someone is waiting for you (especially on days when the weather is bad or you feel too tired), you'll be more likely to show up for a run.

4. Run where you enjoy running. No matter where you live, you can find somewhere enjoyable to run. Don't get stuck in a rut and run only on sidewalks or near busy streets all

the time. Search out trails, dirt paths, playing
fields or county and city parks. Enjoy where
you run.

Steve Scott is a three-time Olympian and the American record holder in the mile. He has run more
than 135 sub-four-minute miles. Steve is the cross-country coach at Cal State San Marcos, San
Marcos, CA.

"The champ may have lost his stuff

temporarily or permanently,

he can't be sure.

When he can no longer throw

his high hard one,

he throws his heart instead.

He throws something.

He just doesn't walk off the mound

and weep."

RAYMOND CHANDLER

My Danny DeVito
Motivation

I'm a 5'7," 135-pound male with a marathon PR of 3:11. I motivate myself to run by thinking of my "Danny DeVito motivation":

"While I'm destined to be short, and accept that fact, I don't want to be short and fat like Danny DeVito."

That thought keeps me on a pretty consistent training plan.

Scott Angel
Charlotte, NC

"The secret of discipline is motivation.
When a man is sufficiently motivated,
discipline will take care of itself."
SIR ALEXANDER PATERSON

Wife, Mother, Runner,

Olympic Trials Qualifier...

What makes Lisa Run?

LISA VALENTINE'S STORY

Don't tell Lisa Valentine that a mother of five children can't possibly qualify for the Olympic
Marathon Trials. Don't even suggest that someone
with only three years' running experience could
not compete against women who've trained for
years. And don't ever try to convince her that
most elite runners start running when they're in
their twenties, not their mid-thirties. Lisa defies
the odds, and, graciously and modestly, acknowledges her achievements.

"Without the support of my husband, who
watched our children while I ran, my terrific
coach, and my training mates, I would never have
broken three hours in my first marathon. I quickly learned that running can be a solitary, lonely

sport. If you want to get better, you have to find other people who share your passion."

"You're never too old to start; I'm proof of that."

Lisa's newfound passion took her all the way to the 2000 Women's Olympic Marathon Trials. On a warm, humid day she ran 2:55:28, good enough for seventy-fifth overall. The Trials race was only her fourth marathon.

"I didn't start out as a runner. It was my second choice. First was the Stairmaster. In fact, members of the health club where I worked out used to call me 'Queen of the Stairmaster!'" In 1997, when Lisa was thirty-five, her husband, Dwight, suggested she take up running, an activity she hadn't indulged in since high school. "Even though we had four kids at the time, and I was working out several times a week, I still had a lot of energy." She certainly did have 'a lot of energy,' enough energy, in fact, to take second place in her first race, a 5K close to her St. Petersburg home. "After running well in another big race here in town, I decided that maybe I should try a marathon. I knew I couldn't do it alone, though. I needed help scheduling my time, and I needed to learn all I could about running."

In rapid succession Lisa joined a running club,

located a coach and found training partners. "My overall win in the Tucson Marathon that qualified me for the Olympic Trials was even more exciting because my training partner finished second and also qualified. We ran all our long runs together. For a month we met at 4:30 a.m., so we'd have time to get in our run before my kids woke up. After a while we started getting tired, so we moved the time forward to 5:00 a.m."

Although Lisa ran as many as 100 miles each week while training for the Trials, she maintained a clear-headed perspective on how to integrate running into her life. "You have to have a healthy attitude. I've learned to fit my running in around my family, not the other way around. I take my kids to races with me. Before my husband bought me a treadmill for training at home, I used a babysitting service at the gym. I've always made sure to start my long runs early enough that I'll be home when my kids wake up. Without my husband's support, I couldn't have achieved what I've done. Running is a wonderful hobby, but my family comes first."

Lisa is looking forward to turning forty and breaking some masters' records. "You're never too old to start; I'm proof of that. Maybe you're someone who doesn't realize you could be a good runner. You've got nothing to lose by trying. Find other people to run with, and feed off the successes of your training partners. Read as much as you can about training and racing, seek out role models, and work with a coach. Above all, maintain a sense of balance in your life. I found the runner inside me. You can too!"

Postscript: Lisa dedicates her runs and all her races to her mother, who died of diabetes at the age of forty-eight.

"*This is the beginning of a new day.*
    God has given me this day to use as I will.
  I can waste it or use it for good,
        but what I do today is important,
because I am exchanging a day of my life for it!
  When tomorrow comes,
      this day will be gone forever,
    leaving in its place something
      that I have traded for it.
        I want it to be gain, and not loss;
  good, and not evil;
success, and not failure;
      in order that I shall not regret
      the price I have paid for it."

ANONYMOUS

"Slowing Down Fast!"

Hi! This is Bill Rodgers. Hmmmmm...the Big "M," huh? Motivation. Well, I've learned over the years that it ebbs and flows. Not always positive, but usually. I find that I get something positive out of almost every race. I guess it's the friendship, the goodwill and the good vibes that happen at road races.

I do struggle with the aging thing, and all that it means. Sometimes it's tough when you're an athlete aiming for certain goals and trying to stay fit. The Running Quest is an amazing thing. I know I'm doing the right thing by continuing to run. The tough question is racing! I answered part of that question by retiring from competitive marathoning and I reduced my total training to a level I can psychologically and physiologically sustain.

See you on the roads!

Slowing down fast — Bill Rodgers

Bill Rodgers is a four-time winner of the Boston and New York City Marathons. In 1995, he took first place in the masters division in fifteen races. In 1998, he took first place in the 50–54 age group in all (twenty-nine) races he ran. He's the most popular and widely recognized distance runner in the world.

It's a Good Life

In 1997, life was pretty good. I'd just gotten married, and after a long slump in my running career, things had suddenly started to click again. I started to train with renewed focus and energy.

Shortly after returning from our honeymoon, I found a little bump just above my right breast. When I showed it to my husband, he suggested I have it checked out. However, I was healthy, running fast and feeling great, so I figured it didn't mean anything. Besides I was nearly thirty-five, and I'd started to notice I was getting more brown spots, as well as hair occasionally appearing in strange areas (like above my lip). I figured everything was part of the aging process and okay by me, as long as I wasn't growing a big, ugly wart on my nose!

As I began to train harder, I started losing weight and the bump became more prominent. Sometimes in the evening, watching television, I'd find myself running my finger over the small, raised area. Whenever my husband saw me doing this, he'd tell me to make an appointment with my doctor. Finally, I accepted his suggestion.

"Running sustained me."

It was good news! My mammogram clearly showed a mass, but the doctor said it was benign. At the time, I remember thinking, "How could the results have been any different?" After all, I was running the Boston Marathon in a few weeks. At the finish of the race, my husband was there, camera in hand. His finish-line photo of my 1998 Boston Marathon captured my pure elation and joy. My life was perfect, and I knew there would be even greater running in my future.

But the bump was still there. It wasn't any larger than when I'd first discovered it, but it was clearly visible. I returned to my doctor, and this time she suggested that to give myself piece of mind, I should have it removed. The surgeon she referred me to spotted a similar bump on my shin and joked, "Well, we could make it a two for one and take care of this one, too." Since I regularly nicked my leg shaving, I figured, what the heck; why not get it over with all in one sitting? Besides, it was going to be easy and only amounted to an outpatient surgery, a local anaesthetic and a few stitches. I'd be up and running again in a couple of days.

To be able to run again soon was especially important because I'd managed to get one of the coveted spots in the Falmouth Road Race. It was going to be "girls' weekend" out with five of us women together in one hotel room. We were planning a weekend of serious fun and some fast running to boot.

On the morning of July 29, 1998, I put on my running shoes for a quick six miles before surgery. It was an unusually cool summer morning, so I ran fast, finished the six miles, and my husband then drove me to the hospital. The surgery was over with pretty quickly. We both felt confident and weren't worried. After all, we'd been told that everything was okay.

"...work a little harder, dig a little deeper, be tougher and have a little more faith."

After the procedure, we met the surgeon in his office. He sat down behind his desk, looked me straight in the eye, and said, "It's bad." Just like that. I don't know how to describe what went through my mind. It was kind of like when a long-time relationship suddenly ends, and you're the surprised party. Or it was like getting a phone call, and the person on the other end tells you that something bad has happened to someone close to you. Suddenly I heard myself say, "I can't run Falmouth." My voice was flat. The surgeon didn't quite understand, so I explained to him what Falmouth was all about. He told me I had much bigger things to worry about, but Falmouth was all that was on my mind. I was caught in a one-thought loop: I can't run Falmouth. That's what the doctor was saying. Then I felt sick.

"Running gave me hope."

What followed seemed like sheer insanity. I underwent test after test and then more surgery to make sure the cancer hadn't spread. On August 5, I had a lumpectomy with lymph node sampling. My lymph nodes weren't affected, but I still was scheduled for six weeks of radiation therapy just to make sure. I didn't run Falmouth.

Instead, I started spending time learning as much as I possibly could about my disease. And I became angry, angry for what had happened to me, angry that I, who was a non-smoker, ate well, exercised regularly and had no appreciable risk factors, had fallen victim to cancer. My anger turned to action. I decided the disease wasn't going to get me. Cancer wasn't going to interrupt my running again. Exactly three weeks after surgery, I ran six miles. From that moment on I ran every other day, and, on September 5, I made a comeback to the racing scene on a hilly 5K course, running 20:59. But I still had radiation ahead of me, starting on September 14. Radiation zaps the body's energy sources. I was counseled to take it easy, but I was having none of that. Running sustained me. It kept the fear from getting close and gave me some feeling of control over my body. Radiation or not, I wasn't going to stop now. I even bought my first pair of racing flats.

During the fourth week of radiation therapy, I started developing burn-like rashes, then my skin began to ooze. The radiologist thought I was crazy to continue running (and racing) in such a state. Nevertheless, she experimented with different creams to see if they would help. Eventually I learned I could run by slathering cream all over the treatment site, applying a gel patch, and then wearing a tight cotton bra to minimize chafing. It was a difficult time. During the fifth week of treatment, I ran a total of nine miles, six at the beginning of the week and a 5K at the end.

After six weeks, to celebrate the end of radiation, I signed up for my first post-treatment 5K. First place was $100 — a nice prize. The race was the weekend following my last treatment. Shortly after the race started, a woman bolted to the lead. I followed behind, trying hard to catch her. By the first mile, I'd drawn alongside her, but could feel the effects of both the radiation and my lack of training. During the next half-mile, we battled for the lead. With a little over a mile to go, I recalled something my husband had always told me, "If you pass, pass decisively." So I gathered up all my strength, sprinted by her, and put some distance between us. But it felt like I had done too much. My legs hurt, and I was breathing hard. And suddenly I had doubts whether I would even finish.

That's when I reverted back to my old childhood prayers. I prayed to God to let me have this win. Because a win would be a triumph over cancer and a confirmation of my health, I promised him that, if I could win, I'd give the money to charity. I'm not really sure what happened then. I don't think it's possible to bribe God, but, once I'd let go of the money, I felt renewed energy. I relaxed, and, with 200 meters to go, saw my husband standing there, urging me on. When I finished first, he gave me the biggest hug ever. Neither one of us will ever forget the joy we felt at that moment. The $100 went to the Inova Cancer Center in Alexandria, the hospital where I'd received my treatments.

It has been two years since I was first diagnosed. I followed my winning 5K with a spectacular year of running. I achieved PRs at nearly every distance and twice won the survivor's category in the Washington, D.C. Race for the Cure. I'm healthy now, even though my body has finally demanded I give it some much-needed rest.

"I'm not any braver or more courageous than the next person, but running gave me the strength to not focus too much on the 'what if?'"

Yet, if I had to do it all over again, I wouldn't change a thing. I'm not any braver or more courageous than the next person, but running gave me the strength to not focus too much on the "what if?" I didn't worry whether I would see my daughter through adolescence and adulthood. I didn't think about whether my husband and I would spend our "golden years" together. After my body had betrayed me, running helped me persevere and gain back some feeling of control. Running gave me hope.

I don't care much for the word "survivor." When I'm dying in my bed of old age, I'll believe then that I've survived. First and foremost, I'll always be a runner, a runner thankful to all those who made my achievements possible, including my husband, who gave me his untiring support and unselfish love, my family members, my friends, my colleagues and people I didn't even know who provided me with incredible encouragement. My coach, John Cook, who taught me to work a little harder, dig a little deeper, be tougher and have a little more faith. And, of course, there's my daughter, Madeleine, who has always believed that her mom could win any race.

Suzanne Nearman
Alexandria, VA

Susanne Nearman lives with her husband, Steve, daughter, Madeleine, resident rabbit Sammi, and cat, Jazzy. She's looking forward to her masters' running career.

"Do you know that disease and death
must needs overtake us,
no matter what we are doing?...
What do you wish to be doing
when it overtakes you?...
If you have anything better to be doing
when you are so overtaken,
get to work on that."

EPICTETUS

A Tough, but Feminine, Survivor

What helps me get out the door during a cold, dark winter day is simply the feeling of well-being I experience after a run. Running has given me mental strength as well as physical; particularly training for and running a marathon. I learned from my first marathon experience that I can accomplish whatever I set my mind to do. I learned that no matter how scary and lonely change might be, I can make changes and succeed.

"Nothing seems too far nothing seems unreachable."

I'm a forty-four year old masters runner. This is my second season of racing, before this I was a recreational runner/jogger for six years. Running was a cheap way for me to get exercise and relieve the stress of raising three young children. Then two years ago I went through a divorce.

Running, and now racing, has kept me sane through my divorce, a painful breakup with a boyfriend, continuing post-divorce issues and my mom's diagnosis of ovarian cancer. I've made many new friends and have discovered my potential. Before my divorce I was a stay-at-home mom with no full-time job experience, taking care of my kids, the house and the garden. I initiated the divorce, found a good job, moved out of the house and started over to rebuild my life.

My lowest moment was spending a weekend in bed, crying. But I forced myself out the door for a three-mile run anyway. Now that I've run two marathons, nothing seems too "far," nothing seems unreachable. Three-hour training runs make me understand that I'm a tough, but feminine, survivor!

Patricia Ryan
Hartford Track Club
Hartford, CT

Postscript: In loving memory of my mother, Mary Lauteri Ryan, who lost her battle with cancer on August 22, 2000.

"We can do whatever we wish to do
provided our wish is strong enough...
What do you want most to do?
That's what I have to keep asking myself,
in the face of difficulties."

KATHERINE MANSFIELD

Oprah isn't Going to Beat Me!

After years of training alone for marathons, I began to do long runs with some of the members of a local running club, and the camaraderie rekindled my motivation to train. My tenth marathon was the Marine Corps event in October 1994, but I wasn't having a good day. At mile twenty-five, I "hit the wall" and started walking. Next thing you know, I heard the spectators shouting, "Oprah! Oprah!" About that time, someone surrounded by four Marines ran past me. Eventually, I realized it was Oprah Winfrey, even though I hadn't at first recognized her because she was wearing fatigues and a baseball cap. Right then, I decided that if she was still running near the end of her first marathon, I should be able to do the same in my tenth marathon! I started running again, soon passed her, and ran the rest of the way to the finish. I beat Oprah Winfrey by two minutes!

Ken Puhlkkinen
Lanham, MD

I am Woman...
Hear Me Roar!

THE JUDY MOLNAR STORY

A peek at her medical records not only changed Judy Molnar's life, but undoubtedly saved it as well. During a doctor's visit in 1996, Judy noticed two words written on her chart: "Morbidly obese." The words jolted her world with a mind-numbing reality check: "I realized I was dying."

"...my only real competition was myself."

Up until then Judy hadn't thought much about her weight. A tall, big-boned woman, she had actively participated in volleyball and basketball in school, but had gradually put on weight over the years. That day she saw her doctor, she weighed 330 pounds. "You know how it is when you're growing up, going to college and then getting into the work world. I had excelled at sports when I was young and even went to college on an athletic scholarship, but could never find the time for working out as an adult. Like so many people, I found it easy to eat food out of vending machines instead of preparing regular meals. I drank sodas all day and never got off my rear end except for walking to and from my car! I thought I was 'settling into life,' but suddenly realized I was preparing myself for an early death.'"

Initially, Judy's goal was simply to regain her health. Although she hadn't enjoyed the activity as a child, she started running, figuring it would take off weight the fastest of any exercise. Daily exertion was a struggle; even running around the block was difficult. "Since I hadn't been active for years, I had no idea how to train. At first, my strategy was to try and run as fast as I could, so I'd tire quickly and get out of breath." She soon decided that saving her life was important enough to hire a coach. The coach suggested she use a heart-rate monitor, and with the monitor, Judy learned to run slower so she could run longer. Weeks passed, and she was running farther and farther; far enough that she decided to enter a local 5K.

"I was so proud of myself running in that race. Even though I was running really slowly, I was out there; I was doing it! Then I overheard a couple behind me. The guy was saying to his partner, 'You aren't going to let that fat woman beat you, are you?' It hurt, but made me so much more determined to finish. That's when I learned that I shouldn't mentally beat myself up and that my only real competition was myself." Judy finished the 5K and then another. Those races led to 10Ks, a half-marathon and eventually a triathlon. As more and more people were inspired by her accomplishments, she began to attract widespread media attention. Judy's accomplishments also captured the attention of the organizers of the Ironman Triathlon, and they invited her to compete in their 1998 event.

"...just because you don't reach your goal, doesn't mean you stop trying."

At that race, Judy found herself in the spotlight. Since she was scheduled to be one of the featured athletes in the "up close and personal" segment of the television coverage, a camera crew shadowed her everywhere. Even for Ironman standards, the weather was grueling. The strong winds forced her to drop out during the bike portion of the event. "It was so hard for me to drop out, particularly because there were some people who'd said I didn't belong there in the first place. However, I learned a valuable lesson from the experience: I learned that, just because you don't reach your goal, doesn't mean you stop trying. I learned that not reaching a goal is not failing. After all, what is failure? Was I a failure because I didn't finish a race? No! When I looked back at where I'd started from two years earlier, I knew I wasn't a failure. Far from it."

Not only did Judy return to finish the 1999 Ironman, she has since competed in numerous shorter distance triathlons around the country and is a nationally known motivational speaker and coach. She's a busy lady; besides writing a book about her experiences, answering questions on her Web page, coaching other women via e-mail, and making personal appearances at events around the country, she maintains a rigorous competitive schedule. During the next year, she'll compete in two marathons and another Ironman.

Judy is delighted to see more and more large women getting involved in running and triathlons. She tells them that it isn't important to be skinny. "What matters is being healthy and fit. It's okay to be different. If you look around at the start of a race and see that you're the heaviest woman there, don't worry! You're not competing with anyone but yourself."

Working with other runners, Judy provides on-going motivation. She acknowledges that it often isn't easy to be self-motivated. "We're a society that spends far too much time on our butts! It's hard to break away from that. Sometimes people will even try to sabotage your efforts to change your life. Ignore them. If you have to, turn their comments back on them. Make sure you have a strong support group, and once you've found one, tell them all about what you're doing. Write out your goals on slips of paper and put them all over the house where you're bound to see them — Like on your mirror!"

"*I'm strong. I'm fit. I'm healthy. I'm me, and I love it!*"

When Judy realizes what she's accomplished in just a few short years, she says she sometimes has to stop and catch her breath. "If anyone had told me five years ago that I'd be where I am today, I would've laughed at them. Now I'm part of something larger than I ever could have realized. I'm a member of a unique community of runners and triathletes. I'm healthier than I've ever been, but I'm not a skinny, pale little waif of a woman! I'm strong. I'm fit. I'm healthy. I'm me, and I love it!"

Judy Molnar lives and trains with her fiancée in San Diego, California. She has written a book, "You Don't Have to be Thin to Win." Her Web page address is www.judymolnar.com.

The Best News
in the World

Todd & Gay

Three days before the 2000 Shamrock Marathon in Virginia Beach, Virginia, Todd Kampfmueller sent the following e-mail to his sister Gay:

As of today, here is a listing of my ailments:

- •Left foot — possible tendonitis; been hurting since October, nothing new
- •Right foot — possible plantar whatever it's called; feeling better than before
- •Right hamstring — still very tight since the 20 miler
- •Chest — beginning of some sort of cold, probably be a lot worse by Saturday
- •Nose — running (see chest above)
- •Left foot — athlete's foot fungus growing on bottom of foot and little toe
- •Right foot — athlete's foot fungus growing on big toe
- •Crotch — chafed, probably jock itch
- •Head — cracked (for even attempting something so stupid as running a marathon)

I'm sure many more will pop up by Saturday.
Remember, it's not too late to bag it and run the 8K!

Love you,
Todd

Despite his misgivings, they didn't bag it; instead, brother and sister finished hand-in-hand in a time of 4:33. Yet Todd had good reason to be concerned, because his sister Gay wasn't in the best of health. Three years earlier she'd undergone brain surgery for the removal of a tumor. During the surgery, the membrane covering her brain was replaced with the pericardial membrane from a cadaver, and a portion of her skull was replaced with Plexiglass.

Her recovery was long and painful; even jets flying overhead caused her head to ache. Despite the pain, Gay had started walking again soon after the surgery, and occasionally even managed a little "one-two-three jog step." However, when she tried to jog more energetically, a "squishing" sound became worrisome. This sound came from inside her skull, and, according to her doctor, was because of air that hadn't dissipated from the surgery. When the sound became too alarming, she stopped jogging and instead settled for walking. For months she continued walking on a daily basis, and, finally, in March 1999, for the first time since the surgery, Gay ran three miles without stopping. Relatively speaking, she was back on track. Not only was Gay recovering from major brain surgery, but she was also dealing with the day-to-day pain and fatigue caused by systemic lupus.

Lupus is an inflammatory, auto-immune disease that affects many bodily systems, including skin, joints and internal organs. Extreme fatigue, severe joint pain and swelling, arthritis, muscle aches, weight loss, skin rashes and nausea all character-ize the disease. Lupus causes the body to produce antibodies against its own cells. These antibodies cause chronic diseases by fighting against the body's blood cells, organs and tissues. Although medications can relieve some lupus symptoms, doctors don't know what causes the disease, and there is no known cure. Lupus is a chronic disease that can vary from episodes of illness to a fatal dis-ease. Usually one organ system is initially involved, but additional organs often become involved later. Many people with lupus find it dif-ficult to get through the day because of the pain; often they can't even get out of bed. Yet Gay ran a half-marathon just a week before she first saw her doctor because of "bone-numbing fatigue."

"Relatively speaking, she was back on track."

Physical activity has always been a big part of Gay's life. She's a Physical Education major who played adult softball and soccer for years before starting to run road races in the late seventies. After watching her brother compete in triathlons for several years, she decided she would do one herself. Unfortunately, a hysterectomy in 1995 delayed her triathlon debut. Once her surgeon gave her the okay, she began training again, but soon began to realize "something was very wrong." She was constantly fatigued and experienced tiredness unlike any she'd ever felt before in her life. Despite the fatigue and accompanying pain in her joints, she finished the half-marathon she had trained for, then made an appointment with her doctor. Gay waited three months for a diagnosis. It came on June 26, 1996.

"He handed me a box of tissues
and continued to explain what I was facing…
I was facing a life-altering situation."

"I remember sitting in the doctor's office like it was yesterday. He told me the good news first; I didn't have bone cancer. Then he told me the bad news; I had systemic lupus. He handed me a box of tissues and continued to explain what I was facing." Gay didn't understand what she was hearing. "There were tears in my eyes. I was facing a life-altering situation. He told me that my running days were over, that I would be on medication for the rest of my life, and that we could only hope I would never suffer major organ involvement. I was so sick then that I couldn't have run anyway, so, when he said, 'No more running,' all I could ask was what I needed to do to get well."

Gay went into denial. She knew she was terribly ill, but refused to accept that life as she had known it was over. She got involved with an association for people suffering from lupus, an experience that was both humbling and frightening. "I saw people at meetings who were in wheelchairs, people who were so sick that their lives were basically over. I decided that wasn't going to be me; that wasn't how I was going to live."

Gay spent the next year trying to control the disease by taking medication and by experimenting with various ways to exercise. Initially she would lose her balance from just walking on a treadmill, but by the winter of 1996, she began to alternate periods of walking and jogging. It was a struggle; after a short exercise session, she sometimes found she couldn't walk at all for two days. She persevered, however, in contradiction of her doctor's insistence that she could only do two to three miles because her body "couldn't handle" any more than that. She started to think again about doing a triathlon with her brother.

She'd learned of the brain tumor in the spring of 1997, and surgery was performed in July – in the summer. "Bad things seemed to happen to me in the summer. The hysterectomy was in the summer of 1995, I found out I had lupus in early summer 1996, and then I had the brain surgery in the summer of 1997." For five years Gay had promised Todd that she would do the triathlon with him. An obstacle had stood in her way three years in a row, but she was determined to overcome her bad luck.

"You are my hero. Thanks for everything."

When she was finally able to manage running the three miles without stopping in March of 1999, Gay knew she'd be able to keep her promise. If an athlete is sick with a debilitating disease, training for an endurance event isn't easy — but for the next six months Gay trained for the triathlon. Once, while suffering from bleeding sores that covered her body, she completed a fourteen-mile run in 100-degree temperatures. After her weekend long runs, Gay would typically spend an entire day in bed. Two months before the race she also found that she was having trouble breathing on a run. Her doctor told her that the lupus had caused her esophagus to narrow and that she would need surgery. She told him the surgery would have to wait. In spite of the fact that she had to be awakened every three hours to take pain medication the night before the race, Gay finished the triathlon, and when she finished, she picked up an entry form for the Shamrock Marathon.

Three days before the marathon Gay received another e-mail. This one was from her secretary, Dianne Page Alexander.

Hang in there—we are rooting for you.

BECAUSE OF YOU!

- •I got up this morning and ran 3 miles
- •I feel better than I have ever felt before in my whole life
- •I have lost the weight I wanted to lose, and I kept if off
- •I have gone above and beyond all my expectations
- •Beau has shown a pride in me I have never seen before
- •I have become closer to GOD
- •I have taken time out of the day for myself
- •I have more confidence
- •I have energy
- •I have encouragement
- •I have the courage to start things I would never have attempted

You are my hero. Thanks for everything.

Two days after the marathon, Todd sent Gay another e-mail. This one said:

Good morning. You are such a great sister! I'm so proud of you. You were my inspiration to keep training. I could have bagged it numerous times, but, no, I would think of you and say to myself, 'Be like Gay'. What an amazing day. Better yet, what an amazing past 4 months. Hope you're feeling all right today. HAPPY FIRST DAY OF SPRING. Please tell all your friends in the support group that I really appreciated them being there for us. You are truly blessed to have such caring friends. Have a great day. I love you so much. Todd

Gay wrote us in a letter dated April 4, 2000: "The best news in the world is that, just last week (March 18), my brother and I actually ran the Shamrock Marathon here in Virginia Beach, and finished it in 4 hours and 33 minutes!"

Postscript: Gay has had difficulty bouncing back since the marathon. The extreme fatigue began again, and she started on chemotherapy in July 2000. She's "back to square one" now, running two miles at a time.

The "Ten Minute" Rule

I enjoy the daily activity of running, so it's not difficult to get motivated to head out the door. Running is a welcome break from the responsibilities of work and parenting. It's a quiet time to be alone or with close friends.

If I'm not motivated to run on a particular day, I'll look at my log, and, if I've been over-training, I'll take it very easy. I rarely take days off, but there's always an option if I really dread the thought of running. I use the old trick of saying, "I'll head out for only ten minutes, and if I still feel lousy, I'll come home." Of course, I always feel fine after ten minutes!

I motivate myself to run hard in workouts by thinking about why I'm doing it. I focus on my race goals, and I never train hard for the sake of doing hard workouts — the purpose is to prepare to race. I always have a goal race (usually a marathon) or a series of races on the horizon.

The process of motivating myself to train for a race sort of loops back on itself on race day. If I'm feeling sluggish, lacking confidence or doubting that I'm ready on race morning (all common feelings), I remind myself of all the hard work I've done. I say to myself, "This is it. This is why you

got up early all those mornings and pushed yourself in the dark and cold when you were exhaust-
ed from the day. So GO OUT THERE AND
KICK BUTT!" It usually works.

Gordon Bakoulis
New York, NY

Gordon Bakoulis, former Editor-in-Chief, *Running Times*; four-time Olympic Marathon Trials quali-
fier; sixth woman overall 1992 New York Marathon, first women overall 1998 Vermont City
Marathon; marathon personal best of 2:33:01; mother of two.

"If you want to do something
do it!"
PLAUTUS

Even if You Can See Bottom... You Don't Have to Hit Bottom

RICK NAWROCKI'S STORY

At the beginning of each day, Rick Nawrocki asks God for the willingness to do what he needs to do that day, and, at the end of each day, he thanks God for all he accomplished. On many days those accomplishments are truly extraordinary feats of human endurance that few people even attempt. When one learns that he has a debilitating disease involving a treatment as physically devastating as the affliction itself, his achievements appear all the more remarkable. Rick lives by this motto: "When the going gets ruff — cry 'TUFF.' " During his lifetime, Rick has had to cry "tuff" far too often.

Rick lived hard, drank hard and partied hard until he was thirty-five years old. He was a self-avowed "mess," both physically and psychologically. The years of abuse had taken their toll; he was an addict and an alcoholic, unhealthy, out-of-shape, overweight and lacking any purpose in his life. Seeing the bottom rapidly approaching, he presumed his future to be both bleak and short. It was a frightening scenario. In 1990, determined not to hit rock bottom, he pulled himself out of the depths and sobered up. Rick Nawrocki was on his way to becoming a new man.

One of Rick's first goals was to get himself in shape, so he started working out at a gym. His progress was slow; initially he could manage only fifteen minutes of exercise. During the next three years, he worked out faithfully every day, but running hadn't yet captured his imagination. It wasn't until 1993 that Rick discovered the joys of running outside the confines of a gym and away from crowds of people. He began running while camping alone in the Sierra Nevada Mountains and found the experience to be totally exhilarating and freeing, so much so that he ran every day on the trip. When he returned from his vacation, he continued to run and in 1994, after only one year of training, he ran his first marathon. His addictions to alcohol and drugs now gave way to an addiction to running. Rick had fulfilled his dream of becoming a new man.

"Rick Nawrocki was on his way to becoming a new man."

By 1996, Rick had reason to believe he was in the prime of his life. He was healthier than he'd ever been — strong, energetic and filled with passion for his sport. It was during the same year that he first heard about ultra-marathons. They were a tempting challenge, so tempting that he became determined to do one. That year, 1996, marked another development in his life — the onset of occasional lapses of consciousness.

Rick tried to shrug off the seizures and blamed them on dehydration or hunger. However, when he passed out, fell and cracked his head open, he knew he needed to find out what was wrong. The diagnosis hit him like a sucker punch to the gut. He had cancer, specifically non-Hodgkins lymphoma and would have to spend the next nine months in chemotherapy. During the fourth month of treatment, he ran his first 50K race, finished in seven and one half hours, and declared himself "hooked" on ultra-running. He even planned to make a 100-mile effort his next race.

The chemotherapy seemed to work, and Rick went into clinical remission for nine months. He had made it through the treatments by focusing on his upcoming 100-mile race and by telling himself that he would take everything "one step at a time." Running helped him deal with the cancer by dealing with one doctor's appointment at a time and one treatment at a time. Unfortunately, he learned shortly before the race in June of 1998 that his cancer had returned. The news was devastating. During the race, he missed the cut-off point at seventy-two miles and dropped out at seventy-eight. Triple chemotherapy followed, involving three days of treatments in a row for one week every month for the next three months. In 1999, Rick completed two 100-mile races. Unfortunately, the cancer got worse and progressed into B-cell lymphoma, a more serious form of the disease. Tumors, grape-size to the size of a plum, began appearing just under the skin — all over his body. On the condition that he be allowed to continue to train, Rick agreed to an experimental medication recommended by his doctors.

Rick carefully scripted both his training and treatment plans.

He had decided to do "The Tuffest," the Badwater 135, an ultra-marathon race through Death Valley to the Whitney Portals. Not only would he run 135 miles through the desert and halfway up Mt. Whitney, but — after a rest — he would also run to the summit of the mountain. He would run eleven miles up, then back down to the Portals another eleven miles, one hundred fifty-seven miles in total. Training for an event like Badwater is grueling. Participants need to acclimate to the tremendous heat they'll face during the race, sometimes topping 130°, by undertaking long, pre-race twenty- to thirty-mile runs in the desert. To prepare, Rick ran two-thirds of the course over four weekends. He ran unassisted, using a baby jogger to carry all his supplies.

Rick carefully scripted both his training and treatment plans. His good friend, Cathy, a world-class adventure racer, had given him a "passport" from the Eco Challenge when he first learned he had cancer. Her suggestions for dealing with the disease and Rick's prescriptions for finishing races and ultimately curing his disease are built into the passport, transcribed below just as he wrote it:

"CRY TUFF (CURE de CANCER)

Destination BADWATER!

Race #1	1997
	11 Month's of Chemotherapy

Race #2	1998
	9 Month's of Rituxan (John Wayne Cancer Institute)

Race #3	1999
	3 Month's of Triple Chemotherapy

Along with assorted 50K's, 50 milers and two 100 mile ultra's last year. Now Race #4 is a little over 3/4 way complete and looking strong for a good finish!

PASSPORT CONTROL

PC x 1) Being told I need to get a biopsy on my arm

PC x 2) Biopsy and twenty-five internal stitches

PC x 3) Getting through the biopsy and being told I have another form of cancer, B-cell lymphoma

PC x 4) CAT scan

PC x 5) MRI

PC x 6) Waiting to see if I'm accepted for Stage III clinical trial

PC x 7)   Bone marrow biopsy (fourth one)

PC x 8)   Signing waiver and accepting experimental medication (liquid radiation)

PC x 9)   Waiting to see if insurance will cover stem-cell harvest

PC x 10)   Learning how to inject myself with Neupogen Stem-cell harvest approved

PC x 11)   Stem-cell harvesting done on Monday and Tuesday (May 22-23); 3.6 million stem-cells

PC x 12)   Starting infusion of Rituxan

PC x 13)   Infusion two of Rituxan backed with Zevalin (liquid radiation)

(Seventy-two hours in three-foot human contact buffer zone)

PC x 14)   Weekly blood test and visual check of tumors

PC x 15)   Badwater heat training July 4th weekend (temperature in desert 110 degrees)

PC x 16)   More doctor's appointments until day of departure for Badwater

PC x 17)   **COMPETE IN BADWATER 135**, then summit Mt. Whitney"

Sixty-nine runners started the 2000 Badwater. Three days before the race, Rick made the following entries in his diary:

"Just left the oncologist's office and was given the thumbs up to run the race. My blood levels are going up, and things are looking good. Five weeks ago I had experimental liquid radiation, and, three weeks before that, 3.6 million stem-cells were harvested and frozen for a possible bone marrow transplant in the future. But all I can think of is Death Valley. Non-Hodgkins and B-cell Lymphoma have to ride in the back seat for this one."

Forty-nine runners finished the 2000 Badwater. When he finished, Rick wrote this:

"We got into Lone Pine, and Shannon, Kari, Denise, and Ben were all there to meet me. These are all some special kind of people. Denise offered to look at my feet, while my crew got me breakfast again. Here I am, beautiful women working on my feet, eating breakfast, 120 miles into the run, and Ben nudges me and says, "Isn't this GREAT." We smiled. Then, if it couldn't get any better than that, Denise and I made eye contact a few times, and that said it all. She had helped me so much in the prior year to deal with my cancer, and I considered her my Prayer Captain. God really speaks through her to me like no one on this planet. We both knew how important this goal was and how tough a road it was to get here, but, through faith and hard work, I was living my ultimate dream. Our eyes welled up with tears of joy, and I was off up the Portal Road. It was a tough thirteen miles, but I didn't want it to ever end. My crew worked in unison to keep me moving along. Now I could see the FINISH, and I started running to finish with a good stride. I DID IT! 135 miles in 55:04:18."

Eleven runners reached the summit. Rick was one of them.

He wrote the following in his diary:

"Chris decided to stay with me, which was nice since I was getting pretty spacey due to lack of food, water, sleep. He's a real friend, a trooper, a future ultra-runner, I think. Chris and I got to the summit at 1:52PM, 79:52 after leaving Badwater. I would like to thank all the people who helped near the top and at the summit."

Rick now likes to say that he's lived two lifestyles in one lifetime, that one lifestyle ended and another started when he was thirty-five. Although his cancer will never go into complete remission unless he has a bone marrow transplant, Rick believes he's healthier now than ever before in his life. He probably won't have the transplant, because it would interrupt his training for too many months; instead, he's looking forward to

Badwater 2001. The 2000 race was a dream come true, an ultimate goal, and he plans to reach similar goals again and again, as many times as his body will allow.

One of Rick's favorite memories of Badwater 2000 was running for a time with a young Marine who had difficulty and ended up finishing behind him. The Marine had run the event before, and Rick had always admired him. When he saw his fellow runner cross the finish line, Rick, his hands extended in a congratulatory gesture, approached the young Marine. And when the Marine saw Rick, he pulled himself together and said, "Mr. Nawrocki, sir, you're the reason I finished. I knew you weren't going to quit."

"When the going gets RUFF — CRY TUFF"

"Dear Coach,

You've asked me on numerous occasions what
motivates me to run the way I do. You've theo-
rized that it's about being one of just a few
amputees who run marathons, that it's a way for
me to deny my disability. You know that I was feeling stuck in my training, tired of being slow, and
tired of having to work so hard to get nowhere
fast. I also told you that, if I could, I wanted to
beat the current world record. However true this
all is, it's not what gets me out of the house at
5:00 a.m. to run.

Every day that I run, watch the sun come up over
the lake, breathe in the morning air and say good
morning to the resident heron, I revel in the best
moments of life. I feel in rhythm with the earth.
For an hour or so, I feel fully alive and connected.
I am so incredibly grateful to be right where I am
at that moment and I know that no other morning
will be exactly the same. There is such profound
truth and intensity in each act of running. I am
also utterly conscious of the possibility that each
sunrise may be the last I will ever have the opportunity to experience.

I'm always aware that change is endless and that
we never know in what direction, positive or neg-

ative, change will take us, or never know what losses will be associated with those changes. It seems as though most of the significant losses I've experienced in my life happened without warning. As a child, I would one day be living in one place, and then, with no time to prepare, I would be living somewhere else. By the time I was twenty-one, I'd lived in eighteen different places. I never knew what my parents would do at any given time. Sometimes they were fine and safe to be around, and the next time I saw them they were violently drunk. People moved in and out of my life without explanation.

"Every day that I run,

watch the sun come up over the lake,

breathe in the morning air and

say good morning to the resident heron,

I revel in the best moments of life."

The freight train accident I was in when I was fourteen and the resulting loss of my foot dramatically altered who I was in the world. My life changed completely and permanently in a split second. A number of years later, when she was only forty-eight, my mother went to work at the usual time, but then never came home, having died of a heart attack on the way to the hospital.

One day my two-year-old son was fine; the next day he was scheduled for open-heart surgery. Twelve years later, after a clean bill of health, he died without any warning whatsoever. He went skateboarding that day. I was dressed to go out to a New Year's Eve party. It didn't occur to me that, when the phone rang that evening, our life, as our family knew it, was over. I hadn't lived that day with my son like it was our last. I hadn't said goodbye to him for real. If my life has taught me anything, it's taught me that we never know what tomorrow will bring. We don't know if we will get a chance tomorrow, a chance to go for our dreams. How I live and love is now shaped by my fairly constant consciousness of death.

"...sometimes I just have to leap in and do more than I should..."

So, this is the real reason why I run. Because I can. I don't know if I'll be able to run tomorrow. I don't know if my eyes will be able to see, or if my heart will be able to feel. I don't know if my spirit will be intact enough to allow me to revel in the sunrise. I don't even know if I will still exist. So, today I run; I drink in the day, and I come home and kiss my children and my husband goodbye with the realization that I don't know if I will ever get another chance to do so. When we all return at night, I feel a sense of gratitude that I can't adequately describe.

So, as we talk about what a successful marathon will be for me, about smart training, and about discipline and pacing, I need to be clear. Running the smartest and fastest marathon comes second to being able to be present and appreciate that I even have the opportunity to be running. And, when you wonder how I can periodically, but predictably, be so stupid as to impulsively compromise my training, my only defense is that sometimes I just can't be practical. Even though I agree with you that it's ultimately irrational, sometimes I just have to leap in and do more than I should because I'm not always able to convince myself that I'll have another chance to do more tomorrow."

Lindsay Nielsen
Minneapolis, MN

Lindsay Nielsen broke the Women's Lower Limb Amputee Marathon World Record in 1997, and then, after losing it in November of 1998, regained it in February of 1999. Now 45, Lindsay holds world records in the 400-meter and the 800-meter sprints, and she represented the United States at the 2000 Paralympic Games. She resides in Minneapolis and is a Psychotherapist and Motivational Speaker.

The closing ceremonies of the 1968 Olympic Games were delayed while officials waited for the last finisher of the men's marathon to enter Olympic Stadium. When Tanzania's John Stephen Akhawari finally hobbled across the line in a time of 3:20:46, he was asked why he hadn't quit. He answered:

"My country did not send me
to start the race.
They sent me to finish the race."